HOPI
History and Culture

Helen Dwyer and Mary Stout

Consultant Robert J. Conley
Sequoyah Distinguished Professor at Western Carolina University

Gareth Stevens
Publishing

Please visit our website, www.garethstevens.com. For a free color catalog of all our high-quality books, call toll free 1-800-542-2595 or fax 1-877-542-2596.

Library of Congress Cataloging-in-Publication Data

Stout, Mary, 1954-
Hopi history and culture / Mary Stout.
    p. cm. — (Native American library)
Includes index.
ISBN 978-1-4339-5968-4 (pbk.)
ISBN 978-1-4339-5969-1 (6-pack)
ISBN 978-1-4339-5966-0 (library binding)
1. Hopi Indians—History—Juvenile literature. 2. Hopi Indians—Social life and customs—Juvenile literature. I. Title.
E99.H7S864 2011
979.1004'97458—dc22

                    2011004134

New edition published in 2012 by
Gareth Stevens Publishing
111 East 14th Street, Suite 349
New York, NY 10003

First edition published 2005 by Gareth Stevens Publishing

Copyright © 2012 Gareth Stevens Publishing

Produced by Discovery Books
Project editor: Helen Dwyer
Designer and page production: Sabine Beaupré
Photo researchers: Tom Humphrey and Helen Dwyer
Maps: Stefan Chabluk

Photo credits: Corbis: pp. 11, 14, 16, 17 (top), 18, 23, 24 (bottom), 30, 38, 39 (both); Deacon Steve: p. 34; Edward S. Curtis: pp. 7, 8; Getty Images: pp. 35 (Dave Etheridge-Barnes), 37 (Time & Life Pictures); Mark Turner: p. 25; National Park Service: p 24; Native Stock: 17 (bottom), 24 (top), 25, 26 (bottom), 27, 33; North Wind Picture Archives: p.15; Peter Newark's American Pictures: pp. 12, 13, 20, 22, 26 (top), 31, 32; Shutterstock: p. 5 (Caitlin Mirra).

Printed in the United States of America

CPSIA compliance information: Batch #CS11GS: For further information contact Gareth Stevens, New York, New York at 1-800-542-2595.

CONTENTS

Words that appear in the glossary are printed in **boldface** type the first time they appear in the text.

INTRODUCTION

THE HOPIS IN NATIVE AMERICAN HISTORY

The Hopis are a people of Arizona in the southwestern United States. They are just one of the many groups of Native Americans who live today in North America. There are well over five hundred Native American tribes in the United States and more than six hundred in Canada. At least three million people in North America consider themselves to be Native Americans. But who are Native Americans, and how do the Hopis fit into the history of North America's native peoples?

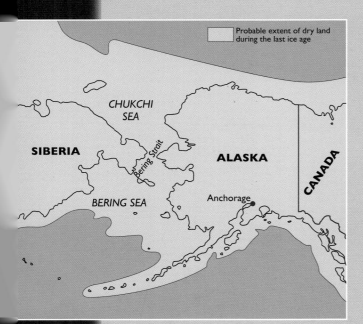

Siberia (Asia) and Alaska (North America) are today separated by an area of ocean named the Bering Strait. During the last ice age, the green area on this map was at times dry land. The Asian ancestors of the Hopi walked from one continent to the other.

THE FIRST IMMIGRANTS

Native Americans are people whose **ancestors** settled in North America thousands of years ago. These ancestors probably came from eastern parts of Asia. Their **migrations** probably occurred during cold periods called **ice ages**. At these times, sea levels were much lower than they are now. The area between northeastern Asia and Alaska was dry land, so it was possible to walk between the continents.

Scientists are not sure when these migrations took place, but it must have been more than twelve thousand years ago, before water levels rose and covered the land between Asia and the Americas.

By around ten thousand years ago, the climate had warmed and was similar to conditions today. The first peoples in North America moved around the continent in small groups, hunting wild animals and collecting a wide variety of plant foods. Gradually these groups spread out and lost contact with each other. They developed separate cultures and adopted lifestyles that suited their **environments.**

SETTLING DOWN

Although many tribes continued to gather food and hunt or fish, some Native Americans began to live in settlements and grow crops. Their homes ranged from underground pit houses and huts of mud and thatch to dwellings in cliffs. By 3500 B.C., a plentiful supply of fish in the Pacific Ocean and in rivers had enabled people to settle in large coastal villages from Alaska to Washington State. In the deserts of Arizona more than two thousand years later, farmers constructed hundreds of miles of **irrigation** canals to carry water to their crops. The Hopis are believed to be the **descendants** of some of these southwestern peoples. Their oldest village, Oraibi, is known to have existed for more than eight hundred years.

The Cliff Palace at Mesa Verde, Colorado, is the most spectacular example of Native American culture that survives today. It consists of more than 150 rooms and pits built around A.D. 1200 from sandstone blocks.

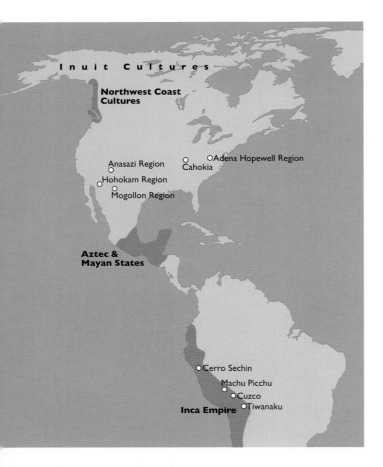

This map highlights some of the main early Native American cultures.

In the Ohio River valley between 700 B.C. and A.D. 500, people of the Adena and Hopewell **cultures** built clusters of large burial mounds, such as the Serpent Mound in Ohio, which survives today. In the Mississippi **floodplains**, the native peoples formed complex societies. They created mud and thatch temples on top of flat earth pyramids. Their largest town, Cahokia, in Illinois, contained more than one hundred mounds and may have been home to thirty thousand people.

CONTACT WITH EUROPEANS

Around A.D. 1500, European ships reached North America. The first explorers were the Spanish. Armed with guns and riding horses, they took over land and forced the Native Americans to work for them. The Spanish were followed by the British, Dutch, and French, who were looking for land to settle and for opportunities to trade.

In the 1540s, the Spanish arrived in Hopi territory for the first time but soon left the Hopis alone. Missionaries followed in the 1600s. Although they introduced metal goods and new farm animals and plants, they had little success in converting the Hopis to Christianity. The Hopis took part in a widespread

This photo from the beginning of the twentieth century shows typical traditional Hopi housing. Family homes were joined to each other, and ladders were used to reach the roof.

revolt against the Spanish in 1680 and destroyed the only church on their land in 1700.

When Native Americans met Europeans they came into contact with diseases, such as smallpox and measles, that they had never experienced before. At least one half of all Native Americans, and possibly many more than that, were unable to overcome these diseases and died.

Guns were also disastrous for Native Americans. At first, only the Europeans had guns, which enabled them to overcome native peoples in fights and battles. Eventually, Native Americans groups obtained guns and used them in conflicts with each other. Native American groups were also forced to take sides and fight in wars between the French and British.

Horses, too, had a big influence in Native American lifestyles, especially on the Great Plains. Some groups became horse breeders and traders. People were able to travel greater distances and began to hunt buffalo on horseback. Soon horses became central to Plains trade and social life.

At the end of the 1700s, people of European descent began to migrate over the Appalachian Mountains, looking for new land to farm and exploit. By the middle of the nineteenth century, they had reached the west coast of North America. This expansion was disastrous for Native Americans.

One hundred years ago, young Hopi women used to gather together to grind corn, the most important of the many Hopi food crops.

RESERVATION LIFE

Many peoples were pressured into moving onto **reservations** to the west. The biggest of these reservations later became the U.S. state of Oklahoma. Native Americans who tried to remain in their homelands were attacked and defeated. A small part of traditional Hopi lands became a reservation in 1882, and the Hopi people were forced to live there.

New laws in the United States and Canada took away most of the control Native Americans had over their lives. They were expected to give up their cultures and adopt the ways and habits of white Americans. It became a crime to practice their traditional religions. Children were taken from their homes and placed in **boarding schools**, where they were forbidden to speak their native languages. On the Hopi reservation, some parents were imprisoned for refusing to send their children to the American schools.

Despite this **persecution**, many Native Americans clung on to their cultures through the first half of the twentieth century. The Society of American Indians was founded in 1911, and its campaign for U.S. citizenship for Native Americans was successful in 1924. Other Native American organizations were formed to promote traditional cultures and to campaign politically for Native American rights.

THE ROAD TO SELF-GOVERNMENT

Despite these campaigns, Native Americans on reservations endured poverty and very low standards of living. Many of them moved away to work and live in cities, where they hoped life would be better. In most cases, they found life just as difficult. They not only faced **discrimination** and **prejudice** but also could not compete successfully for jobs against more established ethnic groups.

In the 1970s, the American Indian Movement (AIM) organized large protests that attracted attention worldwide. They highlighted the problems of unemployment, discrimination, and poverty that Native Americans experienced in North America.

The AIM protests led to changes in policy. Some new laws protected the civil rights of Native Americans, while other laws allowed tribal governments to be formed. Today tribal governments have a wide range of powers. They operate large businesses and run their own schools and health care.

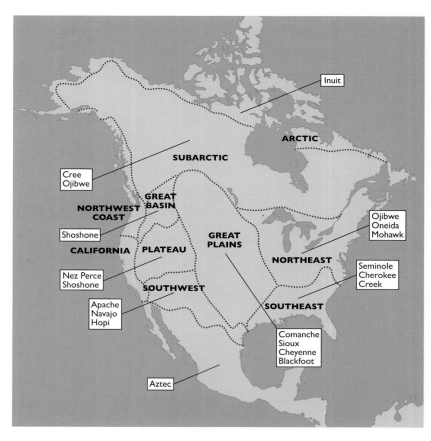

This map of North America highlights the main Native American cultural groups, along with the smaller groups, or tribes, featured in this series of books.

Chapter 1

LAND AND ORIGINS

THE PEACEFUL PEOPLE

The word *Hopi* has been defined as "peaceful people," "righteous," or "virtuous." The westernmost group of **Pueblo Indians,** the Hopis live on a 1.6 million-acre (648,000-hectare) reservation in northeastern Arizona. Slightly smaller than the state of Rhode Island, it is a limited portion of their traditional lands and completely surrounded by the Navajo Reservation. Today, the population of the Hopi Reservation is over 10,000, with the people living in fourteen villages on top of three **mesas:** First Mesa, Second Mesa, and Third Mesa. Scientists have proven that the Hopis have lived in this area for at least a thousand years.

THE TRADITIONAL HOPI ORIGIN STORY

Many Hopis believe that they came to this world, called the Fourth World, from another place beneath this world — called the Third World — long, long ago. According to Hopi traditional beliefs, Tawa, the Sun Spirit, created all the people. Gogyeng Sowuhti, known as the Spider Grandmother, and the boy warrior gods, Pokanghoya and Polongahoya, led the people with good hearts into the Fourth World. Evil people were left behind. The good people climbed a reed through a hole in the sky. They found the Fourth World empty except for Masauwu, the god of fire and death, who welcomed them.

The orange area on this map shows the Hopis' homeland before it became part of the United States.

Called "the oldest people" by other tribes, Hopis have lived for centuries in the dry, open countryside called the Black Mesa in Arizona.

Yawpa, the mockingbird, divided the people into different tribes. After bringing light and warmth to the Fourth World as instructed by Spider Grandmother, these tribes traveled to find their homes. The Hopis settled in an area that is now called Black Mesa, Arizona.

The Hopi Language

About five thousand people speak the Hopi language at home. Here are a few words:

Hopi	Pronunciation	English
tsiro	tsi-roh	bird
taaqa	tay-kwah	man
kiihu	kiy-hooh	house
kwaahu	kway-hooh	eagle
kuuyi	kooh-yih	water
tusqua	toos-kwah	land

Chapter 2

A Long History in a Dry Land

For 850 years, Hopis have lived in Oraibi, Arizona, the oldest surviving settlement in the United States. In Oraibi and other villages, the Hopis farmed corn, using methods that produced successful harvests in a desert land. They mined coal and used it for baking pottery, cooking, and heating. The people built **kivas**, underground rooms, for complex ceremonies created to insure Hopi survival. They also defended themselves against raids by Navajos and other Native American tribes.

The Spanish Come and Go

In 1540, Hopis in Oraibi's neighboring town of Awatovi met the Spanish explorer Pedro de Tovar, sent by Francisco Vásquez de Coronado to find gold. De Tovar discovered the Hopis had no gold and returned to Zuni in New Mexico to rejoin Coronado.

Coronado and his soldiers crossed the southwestern United States in search of the fabled Seven Cities of Gold in 1540 at the request of the king of Spain, who had heard rumors of great riches north of Mexico.

In 1629, three priests arrived in Awatovi and built a Christian **mission** there, but the priests had little effect on Hopi traditional beliefs. However, the people in the mission introduced sheep, cattle, fruits, vegetables, and metal tools to the Hopis.

In 1680, the Hopis joined with other Pueblo peoples in the Pueblo Revolt against the Spanish, who counted the region part of the Spanish Empire in Mexico. Twelve years later, the Spanish once again conquered the Pueblo peoples of New Mexico. Priests returned to Awatovi, causing disagreement among the Hopis. Some wanted to live like the Christians, and others wanted to continue to live in the traditional manner. In 1700, the traditional Hopis killed all the Christian men and destroyed Awatovi. From 1823 to 1845, the Mexican governors located in Santa Fe, New Mexico, failed to stop Navajos and other Native groups from raiding Hopi **pueblos**.

The Pueblo Revolt

Pópe, a **medicine man** of the San Juan Pueblos, organized the 1680 revolt against the Spanish. During the mid-1600s, the Spanish had moved into New Mexico and built missions in all the Pueblo towns. Tired of living with the Spanish people, who treated them as workers and servants and forced them to follow their religion, the Native Americans were ready for a change. Pópe sent messengers to all of the Pueblo peoples, including the Hopis, telling them to fight the Spanish on the same day. Since there were no calendars, Pópe sent a cord with knots showing how many days until the revolt. Although the Pueblos' revolt was successful, the Spanish soon returned.

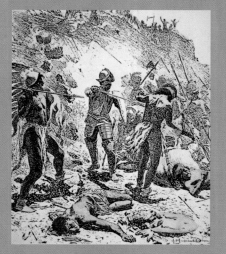

During the Pueblo Revolt, Native Americans killed the Spanish or chased them out of town and destroyed everything that was Spanish.

AMERICAN CONTACT

In 1846, the United States and Mexico began a war over which country held present-day Texas and the location of that state's boundary with Mexico. When the United States won the war in 1848, it gained a vast amount of territory, including Texas, California, Nevada, Utah, and most of Arizona as well as parts of other present-day U.S. states. Hopi lands thus became a part of the United States.

Hopi men traveled to Santa Fe, New Mexico, to ask John Calhoun (above), Indian agent and later governor of the territory, for help in defending themselves against Navajo raids.

In 1849, the U.S. government named John Calhoun to act as Indian agent and govern the southwestern tribes. The Hopis began to meet American missionaries, traders, explorers, government officials, and tourists. In 1874, the Keams Canyon government agency was built, as were three Christian missions. Without consulting the Hopis, President Chester Arthur established a reservation, where all members of the tribe were supposed to live, in 1882. However, the new Hopi reservation covered only one-tenth of their traditional lands.

The creation of a boarding school at Keams Canyon in 1887 had a huge effect on traditional Hopi society. Hopi children were forced to attend the school, where they learned the English language and American customs. During the same year, Congress passed the Dawes Severalty Act, which required Native American tribes to divide their reservation and give each family one piece of land. The traditional Hopis fought against this law, and many of them were sent to prison. In the end, the Hopis kept their reservation whole and did not split it up.

Two traditionally dressed Hopi girls sit in a window in 1900. The American boarding schools did not prepare Hopi girls and boys for their life on the reservation.

Keams Canyon Indian School

The children attending Keams Canyon Indian School were forced to cut their hair, wear American clothing, and speak only English. Separated from their families and culture for years, they were not allowed to participate in Hopi ceremonies. The food and rooms were terrible, and many Hopi children caught diseases and died. Many Hopis refused to send their children, so the government sent soldiers to force the children to go to school and to arrest their parents. Because of the terrible conditions there, the boarding school, which had opened in 1887, was shut in 1915.

Edward S. Curtis's photographs **documented** traditional Native American life across much of North America. He took this haunting photo of a traditionally dressed Hopi man from the village of Walpi in 1906.

A President Values Hopi Culture

President Theodore Roosevelt visited the village of Walpi in 1913 and was very impressed with the people, their lifestyle, and their ceremonies. He wrote about the Hopis, expressing appreciation for their unique culture. In an article published in 1913, Roosevelt said, "It is to be hoped that the art, the music, the poetry of their elders will be preserved during the change coming over the younger generation."

EARLY TWENTIETH CENTURY

During the early 1900s, disagreements among the Hopis created the worst problems the tribe had yet faced. Hopis divided into two different sides: the U.S. government reports named them the "Friendlies" and the "Hostiles." The Friendlies were in favor of learning English and cooperating with the government. Today, they are called "Progressives." Called the "Traditionalists" today, the Hostiles did not want any changes to the Hopi lifestyle.

In 1906, the disagreements between the Hostiles and the Friendlies of Oraibi ended in a fight. Youkeoma, leader of the Hostiles, drew a line in the sand and said that he and his people would leave Oraibi if the Friendlies' leader, Tewaquaptewa, could push him across the line. After a long pushing contest, he was pushed over the line, and the Hostiles left Oraibi to begin a

The traditional Pueblo Indian architecture of Old Oraibi featured an **adobe** and stone "apartment building" where Hopis could climb to the top floor by stone stairs or by ladder.

new traditional village called Hotevilla. Oraibi continued to lose people until it became a dying village of only one hundred people instead of a lively center of six hundred.

The 1934 Indian Reorganization Act provided a way for Native American nations to establish their own tribal government; each voted whether to accept the act. Though most Hopis refused to vote in the tribal election, the Hopi Tribal Council was formed in 1936. The council functioned only occasionally until the 1950s.

Present-day Hotevilla features modern housing funded by the U.S. government.

LATER TWENTIETH CENTURY

With World War II (1939–1945) came an increase in the number of Hopis moving off the reservation. Some fought in the war, while some **conscientious objectors** left the reservation to provide other services to the country, such as nursing, fighting fires, or building dams. Still others left the reservation to work in factories to aid the war effort. Most of these Hopis returned to the reservation more knowledgeable about the outside world.

The tribal council was revived in the 1950s to deal with the outsiders, such as U.S. government officials and other non-Hopis, but the twelve Hopi villages each governed themselves. All but one of the villages favor the traditional Hopi form of government by a *kikmongwi*, or village chief.

During World War II, Private Floyd Dann, a Hopi, spoke to other tribal members in the U.S. Army using a code based on the Hopi language. No one on the enemy side could figure out what the Hopis were saying, making this a useful way of passing information during wartime.

Hopi Conscientious Objectors

The Hopis have always tried to peacefully resolve **conflicts** without going to war. During World War I (1914–1918), only 10 percent of the Hopis served in the armed forces; the rest of the tribe held on to their tradition of peace. Many Hopis registered as conscientious objectors during World War II. Although most signed up to serve the government in ways that did not involve combat, many others were put in prison because they refused to fight. Today, Hopis are allowed to become conscientious objectors in any war because of their deep and long-held tradition of peace.

One of the first things that the new tribal council did was to **sue** the Navajo tribe in 1960. The Hopis claimed that Navajo settlers **trespassed** on the Hopi Reservation as established in 1882 and that the land belonged to the Hopis. This problem became so large that the U.S. government passed the 1974 Navajo-Hopi Land Settlement Act. This law divided the disputed land between the Navajos who lived there and the Hopis who owned it. Hopis who lived on Navajo land were supposed to move to the Hopi land, and the Navajos on Hopi land were to move to Navajo land. While most of the Hopis left Navajo land, many Navajo families on Hopi land did not, having lived there for generations. Both sides are unhappy with the current situation, and **negotiations** continue. The Hopis deeply feel the loss of even more of their traditional lands.

It is upon this land that we wish to live in peace and harmony with our friends and with our neighbors.

From the 1951 Shongopovi village leaders' statement to the federal Bureau of Indian Affairs about the Hopi traditional lands

TRADITIONAL WAY OF LIFE

Chapter 3

HOPI ECONOMY AND LIFESTYLE

The Hopis were farmers, growing corn, beans, squash, and cotton. After they met the Spanish, they traded these crops for animals such as horses and sheep, as well as for peaches and apricots. They also traded with the people from Mexico for chili peppers.

Each Hopi village took care of its own people. There was no **private property**; different **clans** owned the fields along the waterways below the villages. While the fields belonged to the women in each clan, their husbands, brothers, and sons planted and cared for the crops.

The Hopis planted at least twenty-four different kinds of colored corn but most often used the blue and white kinds. Many wild plants growing nearby proved useful for making shampoo, hairbrushes, brooms, baskets, and trays. The Hopis hunted rabbits and other small animals and traded for other goods that they needed, first with other tribes and later with the Spanish and the Americans.

Hopi men hunted rabbits with a curved stick that was thrown with deadly accuracy at the racing cottontails.

Hopi men contributed their work in the fields, the harvests, and their sheep to the household where they lived — their mother's, wife's, or sister's household. They also wove material, usually for ceremonial clothing of white cotton and wool, while the women made pottery.

The women ground the corn and cooked a variety of meals with it. One of the most common foods was called *piki,* a paper-thin bread made of blue corn that was cooked on a special hot piki stone found in every Hopi household.

SOCIAL ORGANIZATION

All Hopi people belonged to a clan, a group of relatives of a person's mother. Hopi households contained just one family but often included the mother's other relatives. Originally, seventy-five clans existed, but today there are thirty-four Hopi clans, including the Cloud, Spider, Snake, Bear, Butterfly, and Eagle clans. Each clan has its own kachina (a form of spirit being) and special responsibilities in the village and during ceremonies. Clan members always knew what their roles in Hopi society were.

Hopi Homes

Attached to other Hopis' homes, the typical Hopi home was made out of adobe. As in an apartment building, walls separated each family's living space, often with several rooms upstairs and downstairs. The downstairs rooms were storage rooms, and the family lived in the upstairs rooms and cooked piki on the roof of the storage rooms. Inside the cool, shady rooms was space for weaving, sleeping, eating, and family life. Ladders on the outside of the home led to the roof, where people could sleep if it was too warm inside.

The left-hand image in these rock carvings at Betatakin, a cliff village in Arizona, represents the Hopi fire clan.

Hopis also belonged to societies made up of members of various clans. There were fewer societies than clans. Members of the societies were leaders for the important ceremonies; they made sure that the ceremonies were performed correctly and that each clan did their part. Important ceremonies such as *Soyal* (the winter **solstice** ceremony) had their own societies to govern them, and all adult men belonged to the Kachina Society as well as at least one other society.

Each Hopi village was independent and governed itself. Typically, the village chief, or kikmongwi, chose and trained the next leader, but the villagers had to approve the choice. Usually the head of the Bear Clan, the kikmongwi led the village, solved

Kachina Discipline

When Hopi children seriously misbehaved, their parents didn't ground them. Instead, when the children least expected it, scary-looking kachinas — carrying ropes, axes, and baskets on their back to hold the children — arrived at the door to take them away. These kachinas told everyone about the children's bad behavior and threatened to eat them. Parents hurried over to give the kachina food to eat instead, and the children promised better behavior.

problems, and worked with outsiders. The second-in-command, the village crier, called out the news and announcements as he walked through the village each morning.

A Child's Life

Families hid their babies from the sun for nineteen days after birth. On the twentieth day, the baby's grandmother named it in a family ceremony. The baby was then blessed with cornmeal and taken outside to meet the sun at dawn.

Children learned how to do things by helping their parents with household work. They might begin by gathering firewood or helping adults pick fruits and plants. Soon the boys learned how to hunt rabbits, grow corn, and weave cloth. The girls learned how to grind corn and make piki bread, baskets, and pottery. Children spent time playing games, such as running races, shooting arrows, and throwing darts. Adults told traditional stories to teach children about Hopi history, religion, culture, and the proper way to behave.

This Hopi mother and child are all dressed up to visit Hopi House. Relatives in the mother's clan also help teach the child how to be a good clan member.

One of the Museum of Northern Arizona's exhibits is a life-sized kiva ceremonial room, such as those used by the Hopis. The Hopis climbed down ladders into the kiva, which represented the world from which the people had emerged long ago.

Both boys and girls were **initiated** into a society at age seven, where they were given another name. The boys were able to enter the kivas after that. When girls were ready to marry, they had a corn-grinding ceremony and put their hair up into a special "squash-blossom" style over their ears. They wore it this way until they were married. **Adolescent** boys had a second initiation into one of four societies — singer, horn, agave, or *wuwuchim* (which means New Fire Ceremony) — sometime between ages sixteen and twenty and began to participate fully in Hopi ceremonial life.

A Hopi girl's hair is arranged into the special "squash-blossom" style that she wore until she was married, when she would wear it loose or in braids. Today, young women wear this time-consuming style only on special occasions.

ADULT LIFE

Women wore a *manta,* a blanket wrapped around them and fastened like a dress. In cool weather, men wore shirts and pants; when it was warm, they just wore **breechcloths**. When it got cold, everyone put on leggings and blankets.

When a man and woman were married, the man's male relatives wove the bride's wedding robes out of white cotton, and the bride ground corn for the groom's family for four days before the wedding. After the marriage ceremony, where the groom's parents washed the hair of the bride and groom in a yucca-root shampoo and everyone had a large feast, the bride and groom went to live with the bride's family.

Kachina Dolls

According to traditional Hopi religious beliefs, kachinas were **supernatural** beings who come to Hopi villages from February through July each year to participate in Hopi ceremonies. They had the power to bring rain, help the people, and punish anyone who deserved it. People thought of kachinas as messengers from the gods.

On ceremonial-dance days, adults dressed as kachinas also brought gifts to the boys and girls. Girls usually received a brightly painted, carved wooden doll that looked like a kachina, and boys received colorful bows and arrows, rattles, or **bullroarers**. The girls' dolls have become popular with tourists and collectors. Today, many talented Hopi carvers create kachina dolls for sale.

Most Hopi men carve different kinds of kachina dolls out of the roots of cottonwood trees and paint them.

The Hopis have a complicated cycle of ceremonies occurring each month throughout the year. This picture, made in 1910, shows dancers in the plaza during a Hopi harvest ceremony, which was probably one of the women's ceremonies in September.

HOPI CEREMONIES

Most ceremonies were held to honor and communicate with the spirits, asking for life, rain, and good crops. In the Hopi desert country, everything depended upon rain, and this was reflected in their ceremonial life.

Organized in the villages, the important ceremonies lasted for eight or more days. The first part of most ceremonies included secret **rituals** performed in the kivas. Involving the public, the second part of the ceremony happened in a central plaza and was more festive.

According to traditional beliefs, Hopi kachinas are spiritual beings, wearing masks like this one, who come from afar to dance in some ceremonies.

Some ceremonies were women's ceremonies, and some were social events. The Hopi societies put on the ceremonies, but certain things could only be done by specific clan members; for example, a man of the Sand clan had to bring sand to make the altar in one ceremony.

Ceremonies started when the village crier called everyone to gather. Many times, offerings of feathered prayer sticks, or *pahos*, were placed on altars and in other sacred places. Many of these ceremonies continue today.

Snake Dance

One of the most famous Hopi ceremonies is the long, complicated Snake Dance. This ceremony begins with members of the Snake Society gathering snakes from the desert and bringing them into the kiva for prayer. According to traditional beliefs, the snakes are messengers to the gods and spirits living in the worlds below. The snakes are washed to purify them, and then men from the Antelope and Snake societies dance around the plaza, holding the snakes in their mouth. At the end of the ceremony, the men release the snakes into the desert. Traditional Hopis believe that the animals bring prayers for rain from their mouths to the ears of the gods and spirits.

Hopi men are chosen to go out into the desert and collect every snake that they come across and bring them into the kiva.

Yaponcha the Wind God

This Hopi myth features the boy warrior gods, Pokanghoya and Polonghoya, who were also in the Hopi creation story told earlier in this book (page 10).

Many hundreds of years ago, the wind blew all the time. The Hopis could not grow any crops, because the wind blew away the soil and all the seeds they planted in it. Eventually, the Hopis asked the two warrior gods for help to stop the wind blowing. Pokanghoya and Polonghoya agreed to go and see Yaponcha the wind god, who lived in Sunset Crater, but first they asked the Hopis for some prayer offerings. They also visited their wise Spider Grandmother and asked her to make them lots of cornmeal mush to take with them on their journey.

The home of the wind god in this story is Sunset Crater Volcano near Flagstaff, Arizona. This is a very young volcano, which erupted in the eleventh century. The Sinagua people who lived nearby at the time of the eruption may have been the ancestors of the Hopis.

A **lava** flow from Sunset Crater. The volcano also has a cave which was once a tube of lava. This cave contains ice throughout the year, and cool air emerges from it. Perhaps this is the origin of Yaponcha's home in the crater?

The gods traveled for four days to reach Sunset Crater, where Yaponcha lived in a crack in the rocks. They placed the prayer offerings in the crack then sealed up the crack with cornmeal mush. Yaponcha was very angry, but however hard he blew he could not get out. And so the wind stopped blowing.

The Hopis were pleased at first, but soon they began to feel too hot and found it difficult to breathe. Once again, they turned to Pokanghoya and Polonghoya for help, and once again the gods agreed to visit Sunset Crater. This time, they made a hole in the hardened cornmeal mush, just big enough for cool breezes to float out and form clouds. At last, the Hopis had perfect weather to keep them happy and to help their crops to grow.

Each year in the windy month of March, the modern Hopi people on the Second Mesa remember this story and give prayer offerings to Yaponcha the wind god.

HOPI LIFE TODAY

Chapter 4

CONTEMPORARY HOPIS

Children living on the Hopi Reservation are raised in a traditional manner in their homes, but they attend regular schools just like other children. Although they learn English, writing, and math at school, they may still speak Hopi at home and participate in the Hopi societies when they are old enough.

All children are involved with their parents in a busy round of Hopi ceremonies and must learn the differences between over two hundred different kachinas.

The Hopis raise their children with a strong emphasis on education. In 2001, the nation set up a $10 million fund to help pay for Hopis to attend college.

Lori Ann Piestewa

Lori Ann Piestewa was the first female Native American soldier to die in combat while serving in the U.S. military. This twenty-three-year old Hopi mother of two children from Tuba City, Arizona, was driving a Humvee, a boxy, armored car, for the 507th Maintenance Company when it was attacked on March 23, 2003, during Operation Iraqi Freedom. Though Piestewa could have driven to safety, instead she courageously drove up and down the line of vehicles, stopping for others who were stranded. A rocket hit her Humvee, and she was killed. The State of Arizona changed the name of a mountain in Phoenix to Piestewa Peak to honor Lori Piestewa.

Even though Hopis continue to live a traditional lifestyle on the reservation, many young people leave the reservation to find work elsewhere. The Hopis are still known for being peaceful people, but young people sometimes take advantage of the jobs provided by the U.S. Army.

Those Hopis who do not have jobs off the reservation might work at the Hopi Cultural Center on the Second Mesa, a modern complex with a hotel, restaurant, and

This Second Mesa woman uses traditional techniques and designs to make coiled baskets and trays for tourists.

many craft shops. Others work at the trading post or for the reservation health service or may be teachers or police officers on the reservation.

The village of Moenkopi has recently targeted tourists by building a large hotel with meeting rooms and a travel center with several stores selling Hopi and other Native American arts and crafts. These projects have created several hundred jobs.

Another tribal business is the Hopi Three Canyon Ranches, created from five smaller cattle ranches. As well as grazing cattle on this land, the Hopis have recently extended the business to encourage the hunting of elk and antelopes on this land.

Many Hopis make crafts to sell to tourists. Men carve kachina dolls, craft silver into lovely objects, or weave cotton. Women of each mesa specialize in a craft: the First Mesa women make pottery, Second Mesa women weave trays with yucca, and Third Mesa women form trays from colorful wicker.

Hopi Arts

The Hopis have always had a rich and varied artistic tradition, which continues to this day. Kachina doll carving has remained a strong artistic tradition among the Hopis, and many men carve these representatives of the Hopi spirit world.

Using an overlay method, Hopi silversmiths cut a design from a thin layer of silver and place it over another piece of silver.

A Family of Potters

One of the most famous Native American potters is Nampeyo, a Hopi-Tewa. Born in 1860, she began making clay pots at a time when the Hopis were starting to use American factory-made pottery. Nampeyo's use of ancient Hopi designs turned the useful pots into beautiful art; her pots are the only ones from that time recognized and collected as art.

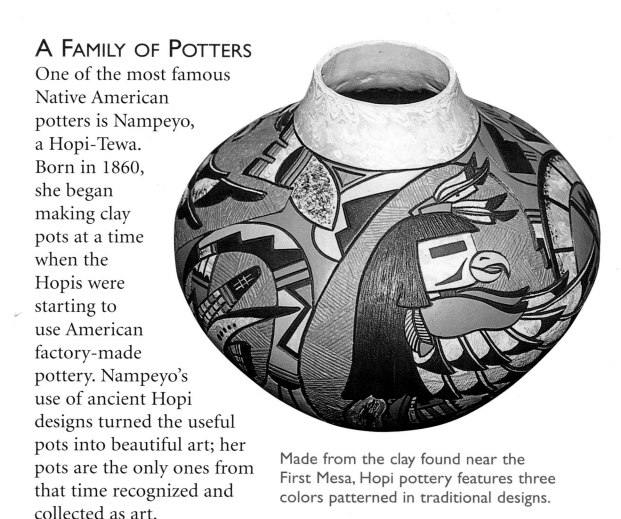

Made from the clay found near the First Mesa, Hopi pottery features three colors patterned in traditional designs.

She was a potter-in-residence at the Grand Canyon's Hopi House and inspired many potters who came after her, including her daughters, grandchildren, and great grandchildren. Her great granddaughter Dextra Quotskuyva is probably the best known of them. She studied and gained inspiration from Hopi pottery designs from the sixteenth and seventeeth centuries. In all her work she used traditional materials, such as dried gourds for scraping and strips of yucca for painting. Where possible, her paints were made from local plants and rocks. Despite the influence of traditional materials and designs, Quotskuyva is celebrated for creating many new decorative ideas.

An Influential Artist

Fred Kabotie (1900–1986) was an important painter and silversmith. He was born on the Second Mesa but had to attend a boarding school in Santa Fe, New Mexico. He began work as a painter of book illustrations in the 1920s, then in 1930 moved back to his birthplace, where for more than twenty years he taught schoolchildren to paint.

Kabotie became known for his murals (wall paintings). In 1933 he was asked to paint the inside of the Desert View Watchtower, which had just been built on the rim of the Grand Canyon. He also joined with his silversmith cousin Paul Saufkie (1898–1993) to develop a new technique and style of jewelry that was inspired by Hopi pottery designs.

Fred Kabotie painted these murals on the inside of the Desert View Watchtower, which is visited by many tourists every year. As well as admiring the murals, the visitors can enjoy spectacular views of the Grand Canyon through the watchtower windows.

Charles Loloma, Jeweler

Born in Hotevilla on the Third Mesa, Charles Loloma (1921–1991) was a member of the Badger clan. He went to Phoenix Indian School, where he worked with painting and **ceramics**. Loloma became interested in making jewelry and experimented with Hopi designs in silver. He used many different types of stones, such as turquoise, diamonds, and pearls, as well as bones in his jewelry. Inspired by the shapes and colors of his homeland, he developed his own unique style. Fresh and new, his work was rejected at some art shows because it didn't look "Indian" enough. Today, if you ask Native American jewelers whose work they most admire, the answer will probably be "Charles Loloma."

SEARCHING FOR ROOTS

Wendy Rose is a well-known poet, **anthropologist**, and scholar. She often writes poems that explain her search for her roots. Her father, a Hopi, and her mother, a Miwok-European, raised her in Oakland, California, in a nontraditional manner. *Lost Copper*, a set of poems published in 1980, was shortlisted for the Pulitzer Prize. Her most recent work, *Itch Like Crazy* (2002), deals with personal and family secrets.

Like butterflies made
to grow another way
this woman is chiseled
on the face of your world.
The badger-claw of her father
shows slightly in the stone
burrowed from her sight
facing west from home.

Excerpt from a Wendy Rose poem, "To Some Few Hopi Ancestors"

Young Hopis like this dancer are encouraged to take part in traditional ceremonies, perform Hopi music, learn Hopi crafts, and speak the Hopi language.

Chapter 5

CURRENT HOPI ISSUES

PRESERVING TRADITIONAL CULTURE

As with many other Native American nations, the independent Hopi Nation faces the very large issue of continuing their traditional culture. Because they remain isolated from today's American culture on the remote Arizona mesas surrounded by the Navajo Reservation, they have been more successful than most tribes.

NO TO CASINOS

Though many Native American tribes have raised money for their people by owning **casinos**, the Hopis have decided not to build one on their reservation, believing that gambling is not the Hopi way. However, these factors have led to a situation where there are few jobs on the reservation, and young people often leave to find work elsewhere.

The dotted lines on this map show the boundaries of the Navajo Reservation, which completely surrounds the Hopi Reservation shown in yellow. The boundaries of the reservation changed in the twentieth century. Land was taken out of it in the 1960s. Then in 1992, more land was added to the reservation, making it three times as big as previously.

The Black Mesa Mine provided jobs for the Hopis between 1970 and 2005, but it also destroyed Hopi sacred sites and polluted and reduced their water supplies.

COAL CONTROVERSY

Coal mining is a **controversial** issue among the Hopis. The Hopis depend upon income from Peabody Energy, which mines coal at the Kayenta Mine on Black Mesa. Peabody Energy is hoping to reopen the Black Mesa Mine that was closed in 2005. Money from Peabody Energy provides much of the tribe's operating **budget**, and the mine also provides jobs. Many Hopis would like to see the Black Mesa Mine reopened. Other Hopis in the Black Mesa Trust want all coal mining to stop. They have taken Peabody Energy to court and are campaigning for solar energy to replace coal-fired generating stations. The tribal council, which supports more mining, has tried to ban all **environmentalists** who are opposed to mining from entering the reservation.

TOURISM AND THE HOPIS

One other source of income — tourism — also remains controversial. Tourists are a good source of income for hotels, restaurants, and kachina carvers, but they are very disruptive to the Hopi lifestyle; many Hopis don't like to have tourists attending their ceremonies and festivities. In fact, some villages have posted signs that say that white outsiders are not allowed in the village or are not allowed to attend Hopi ceremonies.

Hopi Water Crisis

There are no rivers or lakes on Hopi lands; Hopis depend upon rain for farming and wells for their water. They get their drinking water from the Navajo Aquifer, which is an underground body of water beneath Black Mesa. Peabody Coal Company has been mining coal from two sites on the Black Mesa since 1970. Water from the Navajo Aquifer was used to move the coal from the Black Mesa Mine through a 273-mile- (440-kilometer-) long pipeline to be used at a **generator** plant in Laughlin, Nevada. Peabody Coal used 120,000 gallons (462,000 liters) of water an hour, and the Hopis feared that they were running out of water in their desert homeland.

In 2005, the generator plant at Laughlin closed because it was causing too much pollution. As a result, mining at Black Mesa Mine was halted. The nearby Kayenta Mine is still working, but it transports its coal by conveyor and train, not by using the Navajo Aquifer.

Soon, the traditional Hopi farming method of using only rainwater to irrigate crops may not supply enough food for all of the people. Farmers are looking for other water sources.

Former Hopi tribal council chairman Vernon Masayesva speaks at a prayers for peace meeting in Japan in 2010. Masayesva founded the Black Mesa Trust in 1998 to oppose coal mining on Black Mesa and to promote environmentally friendly energy production.

SECRET RELIGION

The Hopis are also upset that some non-Hopis pretend that they know about Hopi religion and try to get money or attention by sharing this knowledge. The Hopis say that their religion is complicated and secret, and they are not supposed to share information about it. The true Hopis are practicing their religion on the reservation and teaching their children about it. They are working hard to keep the Hopi culture alive by continuing their traditional language and religion.

When we take control of our **resources** and begin to develop them our way, there's no need for **poverty** here.

Vernon Masayesva,
solar power campaigner

Today, many Hopi boys love basketball and other sports, but they also learn to run for miles over the mesas in preparation for their traditional ceremonial duties.

TIMELINE

about A.D. 700	Area of present villages is settled.
1000s	Oraibi village is founded.
1540	Spanish explorers arrive in Hopi villages and estimate there are about 16,000 Hopi and Zuni people.
1582	Spanish expedition counts five Hopi villages and about 12,000 Hopi people.
1629	First Christian mission is built at Awatovi.
1680	Hopi population is 2,800; Hopis take part in the Pueblo Revolt that ejects the Spanish from the region.
1700	Hopis destroy the Christian church and mission at Awatovi and kill the Hopis who had become Christians.
1821	Mexican independence from Spain; Hopi lands belong to Mexico.
1823–1845	Mexican governors fail to stop Navajos and other Native groups from raiding Hopi pueblos.
1848	U.S. and Mexican War; Hopi land now belongs to the United States.
1874	Keams Canyon Agency and three Christian missions are built.
1879	Hopi population is 1,790.
1882	President Chester Arthur establishes the Hopi Reservation covering only one-tenth of traditional Hopi lands.
1886	Hopis ask for a school to be built.
1887	Boarding school at Keams Canyon is built; Hopis refuse to divide up their reservation into family plots of land.
early 1900s	Disagreements among the Hopis, who split into two groups: The Friendlies, who are in favor of learning English and cooperating with the government, and the Hostiles, who want to keep their traditional culture and lifestyle.

1906	Hostiles leave Oraibi after a fight and start a new village, Hotevilla.
1913	President Theodore Roosevelt visits the Hopi at Walpi.
1915	Keams Canyon Indian School is shut down.
1918	Hopi population is 2,285.
1936	Hopi Tribal Council is formed.
1939–1945	During World War II, many Hopis leave the reservation to fight in the war, work in factories, or provide other wartime services; conscientious objectors are put in prison.
1950	Hopi population is 3,500.
1960	Hopi tribal council sues the Navajo tribe for trespassing and settling on the Hopi Reservation.
1970	Hopi Nation signs a lease with Peabody Coal Company, allowing the company to mine coal on Black Mesa, in return for money.
1974	Navajo-Hopi Land Settlement Act divides disputed land between peoples of the two tribes.
1998	After mining pollutes and reduces Hopi drinking water, the Black Mesa Trust is founded to campaign against mining and to promote the use of solar-powered energy.
2000s	New tourist facilities are opened in Moenkopi.
2003	Lori Piestewa is the first female Native American U.S. soldier to die in a war.
2005	Black Mesa Mine, one of two coal mines on Black Mesa, is closed.
2009	Hopi tribal council bans environmental groups opposed to mining from the reservation; the issue of mining on Black Mesa continues to divide the Hopis.
2010	Hopi population exceeds 10,000.

GLOSSARY

adobe: sun-dried clay bricks.

adolescent: changing from a child to an adult.

ancestors: people from whom an individual or group is descended.

anthropologist: a scientist who studies peoples and their cultures.

boarding school: a place where children must live at the school.

breechcloths: strips of cloth worn around the hips.

budget: the amount of money that will be spent on something.

bullroarer: small, flat piece of wood attached to a string that makes a loud noise when whirled around by the string.

casinos: buildings that have slot machines and other gambling games.

ceramics: objects made of clay and hardened by being heated.

clans: groups of related families.

conflict: a serious disagreement.

conscientious objectors: people who refuse to become soldiers because of their religious or moral beliefs.

controversial: causing widespread disagreement.

culture: the arts, beliefs, and customs that form a people's way of life.

descendant: a person descended from a particular person.

discrimination: unjust treatment usually because of a person's race or sex.

documented: recorded in written or picture form.

environment: objects and conditions all around that affect living things and communities.

environmentalist: a person who wants to protect the natural world.

floodplain: the area of land beside a river or stream that is covered with water during a flood.

generator: a large machine that creates electricity.

ice age: a period of time when the earth is very cold and lots of water in the oceans turns to ice.

initiated: with a special ceremony, given permission to enter a certain group and share secret information.

irrigation: any system for watering the land to grow plants.

kivas: special underground rooms that are used only for religious and ceremonial purposes by men.

lava: semiliquid rock that erupts from a volcano.

medicine man: a healer and spiritual leader.

mesas: wide, flat mountain tops with cliffs on each side.

migration: movement from one place to another.

mission: a church or other building where people of one religion try to teach people of another religion their beliefs.

negotiations: discussions to reach an agreement on a problem.

persecution: treating someone or a certain group of people badly over a period of time.

poverty: the state of being very poor.

prejudice: dislike or injustice that is not based on reason or experience.

private property: land or objects that belong only to one person.

Pueblo Indians: a group of different Native American tribes who live in the Southwest.

pueblos: Native American villages in the Southwest.

reservation: land set aside by the government for specific Native American tribes to live on.

resources: minerals, land, or other things that bring money to a tribe.

revolt: a rebellion or uprising against rulers.

rituals: systems of special ceremonies.

solstice: two days during the year when the Sun reaches the farthest north or the farthest south.

sue: to take legal action against a person or an institution.

supernatural: beyond the natural world; something that cannot be seen, especially relating to gods and spirits.

trespass: enter someone else's property without permission.

MORE RESOURCES

WEBSITES:

http://www.ancestral.com/cultures/north_america/hopi.html
The Ancestral Art website includes information on Hopi culture accompanied by many historic photographs.

http://www.canyonart.com/kachinas_in.htm
Go to the Canyon Country Originals website for an explanation of Hopi kachinas and images of traditional kachinas.

http://www.experiencehopi.com/index.html
The Experience Hopi website promotes tourism in Hopi country with information about the villages and facilities for visitors.

http://www.holmes.anthropology.museum/southwestpottery/hopipueblo.html
A brief history of Hopi pottery and photos of work by Hopi potters in the Lowell D. Holmes Museum of Anthropology.

http://www.hopiart.com/default.htm
McGee's Indian Art website contains a guide to Hopi kachinas with many images of kachinas and Hopi pottery, basketry, and jewelry.

http://www.indianlegend.com/hopi/hopi_001.htm
A collection of five Hopi legends.

http://www.native-languages.org/hopi-legends.htm
A brief description of Hopi mythological figures plus many links to Hopi legends and traditional stories and to books on Hopi mythology.

http://www.nau.edu/~hcpo-p/index.html
The official Hopi Cultural Preservation Office Home Page includes information on various Hopi crafts, history, agriculture, beliefs, and links to other useful sites.

http://navajohopiobserver.com/index.asp
Visit the *Navajo-Hopi Observer* website for the latest Hopi news.

http://www.statemuseum.arizona.edu/exhibits/nampeyo/index.shtml
The Arizona State Museum website features a Nampeyo Showcase about the nineteenth-century potter Nampeyo. It includes a timeline, the influence of historic pottery on her work, photos of her work and of older Hopi pottery, and an interview with Nampeyo's great granddaughter Dextra Quotskuyva.

DVDs:

Hopi Pottery: A Handmade Heritage. Total Content, LLC, 2009.

Native America: Voices From the Land. Mill Creek Entertainment, 2010.

Books:

Bjorklund, Ruth. *The Hopi (First Americans).* Marshall Cavendish Children's Books, 2008.

Gibson, Karen Bush. *Native American History for Kids: With 21 Activities.* Chicago Review Press, 2010.

Gray-Kanatiiosh, Barbara A. *Hopi (Native Americans).* Checkerboard Books, 2002.

Isaacs, Sally Senzell. *Life in a Hopi Village (Picture the Past).* Heinemann Library, 2001.

King, David C. *First People.* DK Children, 2008.

Lassieur, Allison. *The Hopi (Native Peoples).* Capstone Press, 2002.

Malotki, Ekkehart and Lomatuway'Ma, Michael. *The Fire Stealers: A Hopi Story.* Kiva Publishing, 2003.

Murdoch, David S. *North American Indian (DK Eyewitness Books).* DK Children, 2005.

Price, Joan. *Truth Is a Bright Star.* Tricycle Press, 2001.

Rosinsky, Natalie M. *The Hopi (First Reports).* Compass Point Books, 2004.

Secakuku, Susan. *Meet Mindy: A Native Girl from the Southwest.* Council Oak Books, 2006.

THINGS TO THINK ABOUT AND DO

MAKE A BULLROARER

Get a thin piece of wood that is 1.5 inches (4 centimeters) wide and 6 inches (15 cm) long. Drill a hole in the center of one end and thread cotton string about 3 to 4 feet (0.9 to 1.2 meters) long through it and knot. Take brightly colored tempera paints and paint designs on the wood. When the paint has dried, pick up the string and carefully whirl the wood around your head; you'll be surprised at the sound.

A LETTER HOME

Pretend that you have been sent to a boarding school in a foreign country where they will not let you speak your language or wear your regular clothes or hairstyle, and you cannot celebrate the holidays that you know. Write a letter home to a friend, parents, or brother/sister, and tell them the things that you miss the most.

DEBATE

Divide a group of people in half. One side are Friendlies, the other side are Hostiles. Each person should tell why he or she does or does not want outsiders to attend the ceremonies in their Hopi village.

FLASH CARD KACHINAS

Using an additional reference book or the websites listed in this book, find pictures of about a dozen kachinas. Draw and color pictures of the different kachinas, and paste them onto one side of an index card. On the other side, write the name of the kachina and something about it. Using your flash cards, see how quickly you can learn to identify different kachinas.

INDEX